Science # Book

Springs and magnets

A brief history

TODAY... 1872 In England, James Clerk Maxwell shows how electricity and magnetism are related... 1831 Michael Faraday, in England, and Joseph Henry, in the United States, independently discover how to use magnetism to make electricity... 1823 William Sturgeon, in England, makes the first magnet using a coil and a battery... 1820 Danish professor Hans Christian Oersted discovers that magnetism and electricity are connected... 1750 John Mitchell describes laws about how magnets attract and repel. These are rediscovered and called Coulomb's Laws in 1780... 1676 English scientist Robert Hooke discovers that the more a spring is stretched, the greater the force needed. This is called Hooke's Law... 1665 Isaac Newton develops a law about how the force of gravity works. He watches an apple fall from a tree and realises that the Moon and everything else must be attracted by the same force... 1600 In England, William Gilbert writes an important book on magnets and electricity... 1581 Robert Norman, in England, writes about the Earth as a magnet... 1492 Christopher Columbus makes his first voyage to America and discovers not only a New World, but that the compass changes direction with longitude... 1269 Petrus de Maricourt, of France, describes the forces in the Earth that pull on a compass... 83AD In China, Wang Ch'ung describes a compass...

For more information visit www.science-at-school.com

Dr Brian Knapp

Word list

These are some science words that you should look out for as you go through the book. They are shown using CAPITAL letters.

ATTRACT
To draw towards. If two magnets with different ends (one marked N and the other S) are brought together, they will attract one another and stick together. Objects made of iron or steel will also be attracted to a magnet.

CATAPULT
A device that uses a piece of springy material to throw missiles. The springy material is tied between two posts and then the missile is pulled back with the spring and released.

COILED SPRING
A spring made up in the shape of a spiral coil. If the coils are made with space between them, then the spring can be pushed or pulled. Many coiled springs are made with no space between their coils. These can only be used to pull.

COMPASS
A device that uses magnetism to show which way is north.

LEAF SPRING
A spring made from a bar of springy material. Leaf springs are usually only used in heavy objects, such as cars.

MAGNET
Something that will attract iron and steel and will

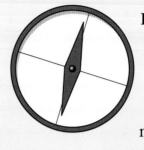

also attract or repel other magnets. Magnets can be many shapes and sizes. The most common are bar shapes and horseshoe shapes.

MAGNETISM
A property of some materials, especially iron and steel, that makes them attract or repel one another.

PERMANENT MAGNET
A kind of magnet that keeps its magnetism for many years.

REPEL
To push away. If two magnets with the same ends (N or S) are brought together, they will repel one another.

SPRING
Anything that can be moved out of shape without breaking, and that will return quickly to the shape it started with when the pull, push or twist is removed.

WEIGHT
A weight is anything heavy. Weights can be added to springs so that you can measure how much a spring will open up.

Weblink: www.science-at-school.com

Contents

Weblink: www.science-at-school.com

Where to look for springs

Springs can be found in many places – you just need to look for them.

What do you think a **SPRING** is? Most people think a spring is a piece of wire made into a coil. We call this type of spring a **COILED SPRING**. Coiled springs can be found in torches (Picture 1), staplers (Picture 2), ballpoint pens (Picture 3), spring balances (Picture 4) and door latches (Picture 5). In this book you will find that there are many other kinds of spring, too.

An elastic band is a kind of spring (Picture 6). It springs back into shape as soon as you let it go.

Even a bent piece of metal can be a spring. Look at a paperclip (Picture 7) or a bulldog clip (Picture 8).

Springing back

As you can see, there are many kinds of spring. But they all share this in common: when we pull or push on a spring it changes shape, but when we let go it springs back to the shape it started with.

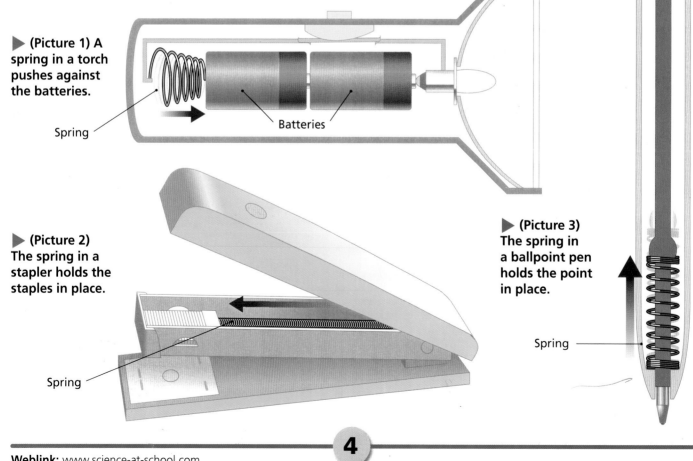

▶ **(Picture 1) A spring in a torch pushes against the batteries.**

Spring

Batteries

▶ **(Picture 2) The spring in a stapler holds the staples in place.**

Spring

▶ **(Picture 3) The spring in a ballpoint pen holds the point in place.**

Spring

Weblink: www.science-at-school.com

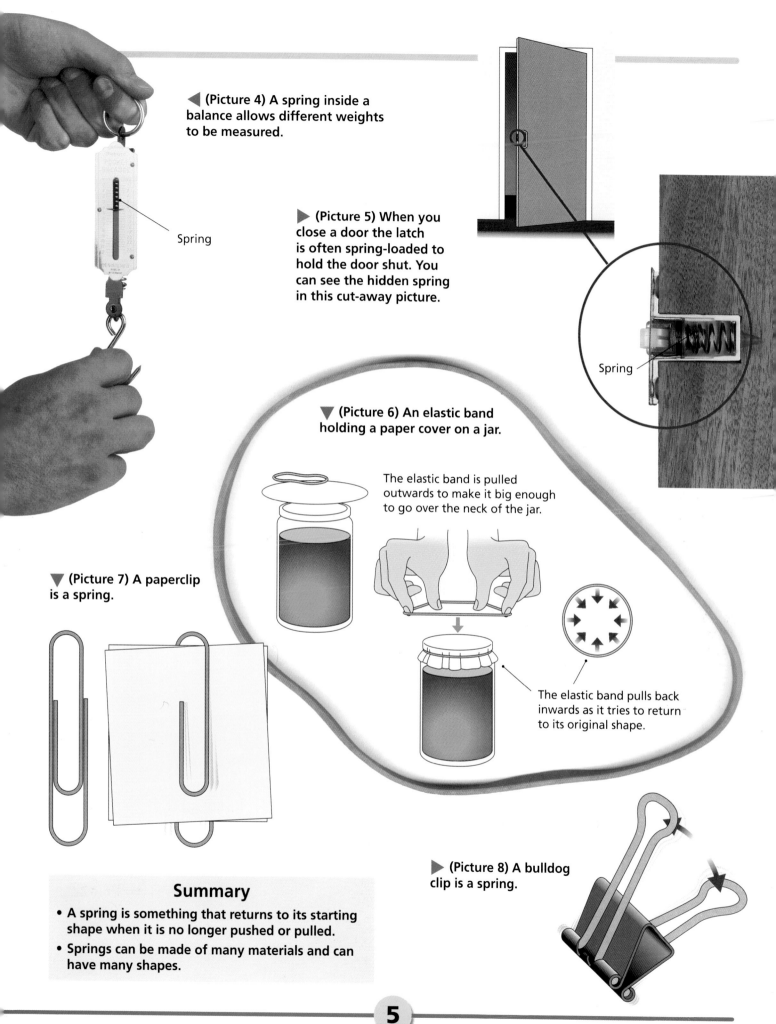

◀ **(Picture 4)** A spring inside a balance allows different weights to be measured.

Spring

▶ **(Picture 5)** When you close a door the latch is often spring-loaded to hold the door shut. You can see the hidden spring in this cut-away picture.

Spring

▼ **(Picture 6)** An elastic band holding a paper cover on a jar.

The elastic band is pulled outwards to make it big enough to go over the neck of the jar.

The elastic band pulls back inwards as it tries to return to its original shape.

▼ **(Picture 7)** A paperclip is a spring.

▶ **(Picture 8)** A bulldog clip is a spring.

Summary

- A spring is something that returns to its starting shape when it is no longer pushed or pulled.
- Springs can be made of many materials and can have many shapes.

Weblink: www.science-at-school.com

Springs at work

Many springs are made of metal coils. These springs can push, pull or simply support things.

Metals are naturally springy materials. But you can make the springiness much more useful if the metal is made into a coil. We call this a coil spring.

How a coil spring works

If you hang a weight on a coil spring the coil will stretch and the spring will pull against the **WEIGHT** (Picture 1). If you push down on the coil it will push back up against you (Picture 2). Notice that whichever way you push or pull, the spring works against you.

Springs that push

There are many kinds of springs that push. The spring in a torch (Picture 1, page 4) is one of these. A clock spring is another kind of spring designed to push (Picture 3). When it is wound up, the coil 'soaks up' the force of the winding. The spring is connected to a set of toothed wheels which are not strong enough to stop the push of the spring. As a result, the spring pushes the wheels and this drives the clock.

▼ (Picture 1) A metal coil that we call a spring will return to its original shape no matter how much it is pulled or pushed.

▼ (Picture 2) These are springs inside a chair. They are strong springs because they have to carry the weight of a person. Each spring is shaped so that it has no sharp points.

The unwinding spring pushes the wheels, which move the clock hands.

(Picture 3) A clock spring is an example of a pushing spring.

The spring is wound tighter.

The spring slowly unwinds.

Springs that pull

Inside a door handle there is also a spring (Picture 4). When you push down on the door handle you stretch the spring, and when you let go the spring pulls the handle back up again. This spring is designed to pull the handle back up again.

(Picture 4) A door handle spring is an example of a pulling spring.

Summary
- Springs can be made to push.
- Springs can be made to pull.
- Springs can be made to support a weight.

Weblink: www.science-at-school.com

Flat springs

Flat pieces of material and long pieces of wire can be used as springs.

You might think that springs are always coils. But there are many other shapes that make springs, too. Even a flat board, such as a diving board, will make a spring (Picture 1).

▼ (Picture 1) A diving board is a natural flat spring.

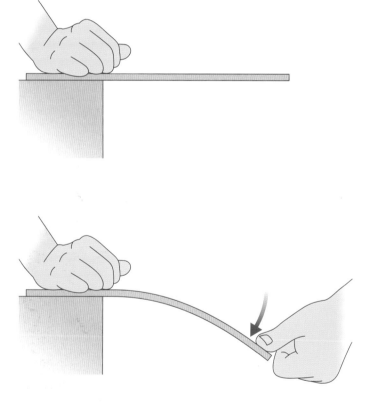

Ruler spring

If you get a ruler and hold it with one end over the side of a desk or a table, you have made a flat spring (Picture 2). By pressing firmly down on the ruler you can hold it onto the table. Then, by pushing the other end down, you can make the ruler bend. If you then let go, the ruler will spring back and become straight again. So the ruler can be used as a spring.

Springiness

Almost everything has natural springiness. If you support a ruler or stiff sheet of plastic between two books, and then put some light things on it, the plastic sheet will bend down in the

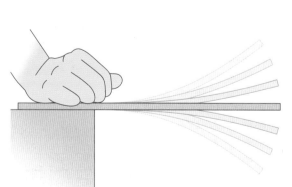

◀ (Picture 2) Most things have natural springiness. When you push on a ruler, then stop pushing, it springs back to its original shape, making a twang.

8

middle. Do not put so many things on that it breaks!

When they are taken off, the sheet will straighten up again. You can see again that the plastic has a natural springiness inside it.

Leaf springs

Because they have natural springiness, flat materials can be made into very strong springs. Flat springs are called **LEAF SPRINGS**.

The stronger the bar, the bigger the weight it can carry and still be springy. Steel bars are used as springs on carriages, cars and trains (Picture 3).

If you tried to bend these springs you could not. But they will bend slightly under the very heavy weight they are designed to carry (Picture 4).

▼ (Picture 3) The wheels in cars, trucks and railway carriages are supported by leaf springs made of bars of steel.

Summary
- Bars of material can be springs.
- Flat springs are called leaf springs.

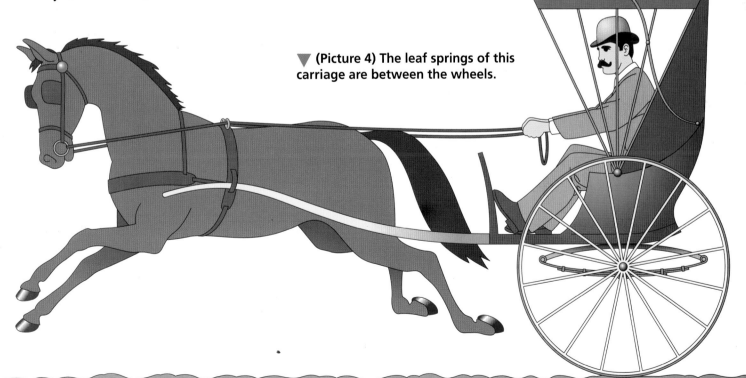

▼ (Picture 4) The leaf springs of this carriage are between the wheels.

Weblink: www.science-at-school.com

Musical springs

If you make a springy material go back and forth very fast, it will make a sound.

Have you ever plucked a guitar or tapped on a drum? If you have, you have used natural springiness to make music.

If a spring moves back and forth very quickly it gives out a sound. You may have heard this if you have twanged a ruler (see Picture 2, page 8).

Elastic guitar

You can make a very simple musical instrument just using your fingers and an elastic band (Picture 1). We might call this an elastic guitar!

Simply pull the band so that it is stretched between your thumb and finger, then pluck at the centre of one side of the band. This will make a twanging sound. Pull your thumb and finger apart slightly and twang again. The sound will have become higher. So, by using the springiness of an elastic band, you can make music. Perhaps you can find out what a whole class using elastic guitars sounds like.

Wire springs and sheets

Many musical instruments make use of the natural springiness of a material to make a musical sound (Picture 2). Springy wires are used to make the

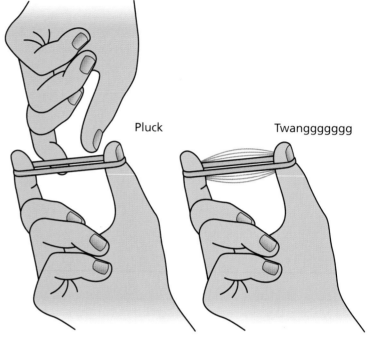

Pluck   Twanggggggg

▲ **(Picture 1) This is an elastic guitar, made by twanging an elastic band between your thumb and finger. It is a very simple musical instrument.**

strings of violins, guitars, pianos and other musical instruments. Springy sheets are used to make drums.

Thumb harp

An African instrument called a thumb harp produces sounds by plucking metal leaf springs (Picture 3).

Summary
• When a spring moves backwards and forwards very quickly it makes a sound.
• A tighter elastic band will give a higher sound.

Weblink: www.science-at-school.com

▼▶ (Picture 2) String instruments give out a sound when you pull on the string and let go. Sometimes you use fingers to pluck the string, sometimes you use a hammer to hit the string (a piano) and sometimes you pull the string sideways using a bow (violin).

▶ (Picture 3) This is a thumb harp. It is made from thin pieces of steel attached to a case made from a gourd. The instrument is plucked to make the steel spring up and down quickly and make a sound.

11

Elastic sheets and elastic bands

Some special kinds of elastic can be very springy, both as bands and as sheets.

If you stretch an elastic band between two fingers you can feel that the more you stretch the elastic band the more it pulls back (Picture 1). You can use this idea to make a throwing machine (Picture 2) called a **CATAPULT**.

Another way of stretching an elastic band is to twist it. You can test how much an elastic band pulls, depending on how much it is twisted, by making a cotton reel dragster (Picture 3).

Elastic sheets

A trampoline is an excellent example of how an elastic sheet can be springy (Picture 4). Have you ever jumped up and down on a trampoline? You are not normally heavy enough to stretch the trampoline much when you stand on it. But if you jump up and down, you push down harder on the elastic sheet.

When you land on the trampoline, you can see the elastic sheet stretch as your feet sink in. Gradually, the sheet stops stretching. Now it has 'soaked up' all of the energy from your jump. From now on it starts to push back, shooting you upwards as it straightens back to a flat sheet.

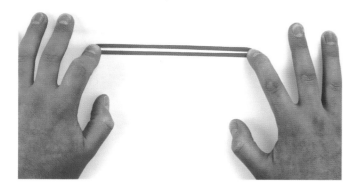

▲ (Picture 1) When you stretch an elastic band you can feel it pulling back as it tries to go back to its starting shape.

▼ (Picture 2) A throwing machine.

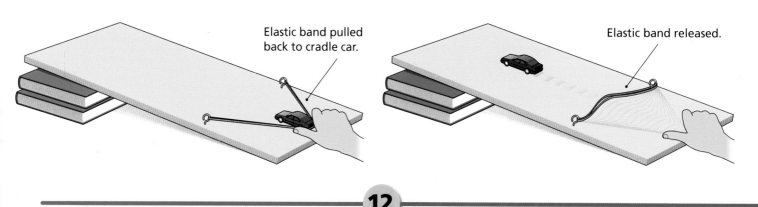

Elastic band pulled back to cradle car.

Elastic band released.

Weblink: www.science-at-school.com

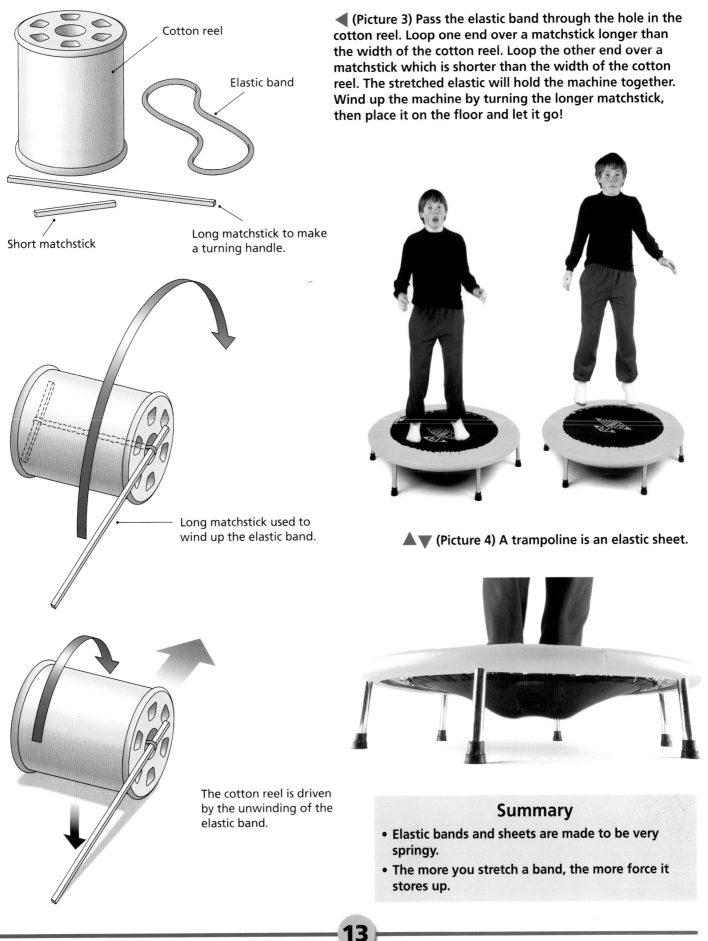

Cotton reel

Elastic band

Short matchstick

Long matchstick to make a turning handle.

Long matchstick used to wind up the elastic band.

The cotton reel is driven by the unwinding of the elastic band.

◀ (Picture 3) Pass the elastic band through the hole in the cotton reel. Loop one end over a matchstick longer than the width of the cotton reel. Loop the other end over a matchstick which is shorter than the width of the cotton reel. The stretched elastic will hold the machine together. Wind up the machine by turning the longer matchstick, then place it on the floor and let it go!

▲▼ (Picture 4) A trampoline is an elastic sheet.

Summary

- Elastic bands and sheets are made to be very springy.
- The more you stretch a band, the more force it stores up.

13

Where to look for magnets

Magnetism pulls and pushes against things that have iron in them.

MAGNETISM is the name of an invisible push or pull that works between some materials.

When things have strong magnetism we call them **MAGNETS**. Iron and steel are the materials most commonly used for magnets.

Many shapes and sizes

The size and shape of a magnet do not change the way it works. So you can find magnets that look like bars, horseshoes, rods (barrels) and tubes (Picture 1). Some magnets even look like wires.

▼ (Picture 1) Here are three common shapes of magnets. They are (A) bar magnet, (B) horseshoe magnet and (C) barrel magnet.

A

B

C

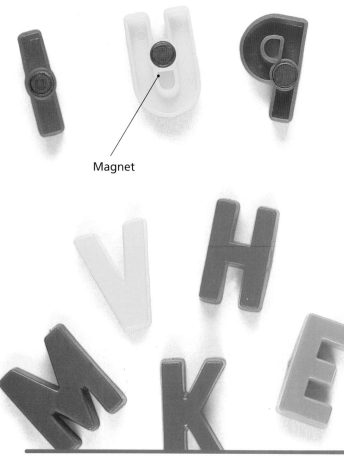

Magnet

Magnets behind the scenes

Magnets are not as easy to find as springs. Many of them are built into things. Look at the magnetic letters (Picture 2). Here a magnet is hidden behind each letter.

There are also magnets in loudspeakers (Picture 3) and in motors (Picture 4). Many door catches use magnets (Picture 5). Fridge doors are held shut with a magnetic strip (Picture 6) and video tape is made of a tape coated in magnetic powder (Picture 7).

◄ (Picture 2) These letters have magnets in their backs so that they can be attached to a fridge door.

14

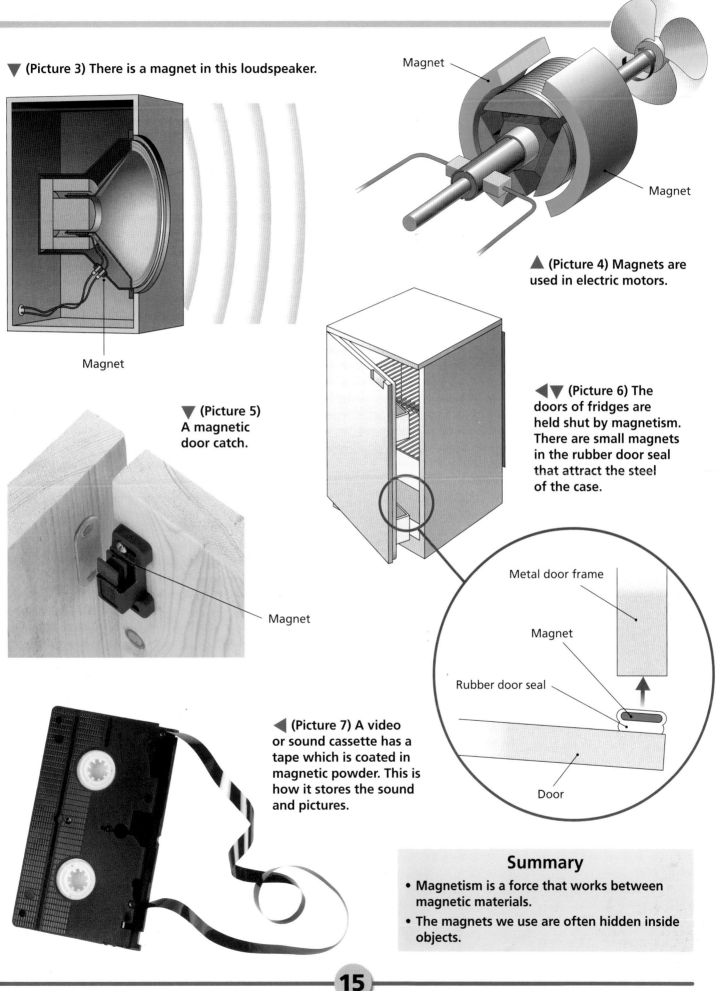

▼ (Picture 3) There is a magnet in this loudspeaker.

Magnet

Magnet

Magnet

▲ (Picture 4) Magnets are used in electric motors.

Magnet

▼ (Picture 5) A magnetic door catch.

Magnet

◀▼ (Picture 6) The doors of fridges are held shut by magnetism. There are small magnets in the rubber door seal that attract the steel of the case.

Metal door frame

Magnet

Rubber door seal

Door

◀ (Picture 7) A video or sound cassette has a tape which is coated in magnetic powder. This is how it stores the sound and pictures.

Summary
- Magnetism is a force that works between magnetic materials.
- The magnets we use are often hidden inside objects.

Weblink: www.science-at-school.com

Making magnets

You can make a magnet – but you have to work hard.

If you hold a magnet over a pile of paperclips, you will find that the paperclips mysteriously rise up and attach themselves to the magnet (Picture 1).

You will also see that the paperclips line up, one hanging from the other. This means that, simply by touching the magnet, the paperclips have become temporarily part of the magnet.

Long-term magnets

You can make pieces of steel, such as nails, into magnets. You simply stroke the nail with the magnet, moving the magnet from the centre of the nail to one end (Picture 2). When you come to the end, you lift it away, then stroke it across the nail again, starting from the middle of the nail.

Do this a few times, then turn the magnet around and stroke the *other end* of the magnet across the other half of the nail.

A nail treated in this way will stay magnetic. It will not lose its magnetism. It is called a **PERMANENT MAGNET**. Now you should be able to pick up paperclips with the nail (Picture 3).

Short-term magnets

You had to work hard to make the nail into a magnet, so it is not surprising

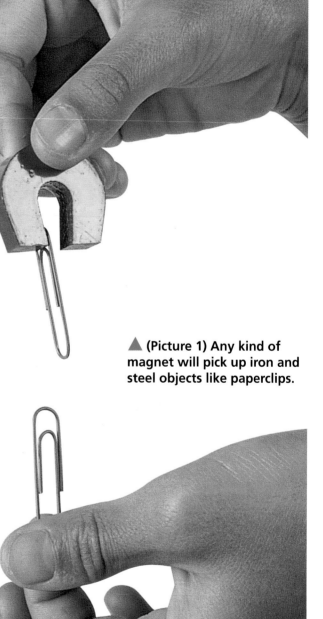

▲ **(Picture 1)** Any kind of magnet will pick up iron and steel objects like paperclips.

Weblink: www.science-at-school.com

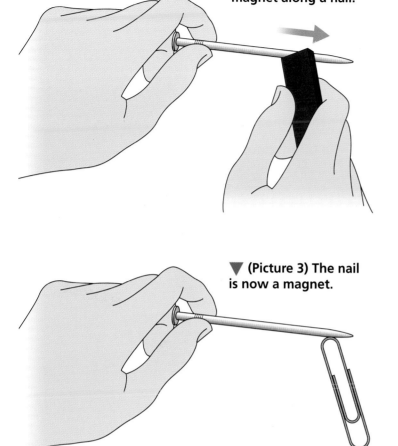

▼ (Picture 2) You can make a long-term, or permanent, magnet by stroking a magnet along a nail.

▼ (Picture 3) The nail is now a magnet.

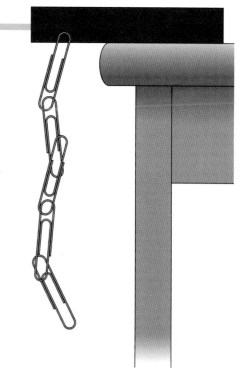

that not everything picks up magnetism quickly. If you place a bar magnet over the edge of a table you can get a long line of paperclips to hang from it (Picture 4).

Now pull one paperclip off the bottom. All the rest should hold fast. Put it back again.

Now take off the top paperclip. All of the other paperclips will fall to the ground. The clips haven't become magnetic at all: they just took up the magnetism from the bar magnet while they were touching it.

▲ (Picture 4) Several paperclips can be hung from a magnet – the stronger the magnet, the more paperclips it will hold.

Summary
- By stroking iron and steel with a magnet you can make a new magnet.
- You do not make a magnet simply by touching iron or steel to a magnet.

Weblink: www.science-at-school.com

Magnets push and pull

A magnet sometimes attracts, or pulls, and at other times it pushes, or repels.

If you bring the ends of two bar magnets close to each other, some very strange things start to happen. Before the magnets touch you will feel either a strong pull or a strong push.

The push can be so strong that you may not be able to force the ends of two magnets together. The pull might be so strong that you may not be able to keep the ends apart.

The magnets you use may have N and S marked on them, or one end might be painted red. The red end is N.

If you try to push two N ends or two S ends together you will find the magnets push back (Picture 1).

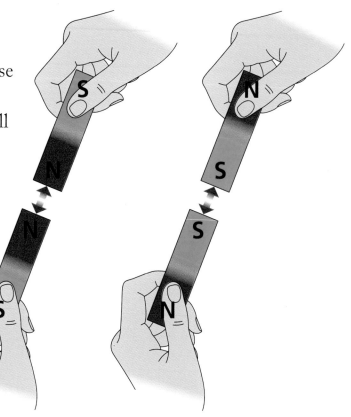

▲ (Picture 1) When you put the same ends of magnets together they push apart.

◀ (Picture 2) When you put opposite ends of magnets together they pull together.

If you bring an N towards an S, however, you will feel the ends pull together and you will have to pull hard to keep them apart (Picture 2).

The rules are:
▶ The same kind of ends push away, or **REPEL** one another.
▶ Different ends pull on one another, or **ATTRACT**.

Magnets work better when closer together

Place two bar magnets on a table top. Have unlike ends facing one another and place them some distance apart, so they do not appear to affect one another (Picture 3). As you move them closer together you will find the attraction gets stronger and stronger. Magnets need to be close together to work strongly.

Magnets work through materials

We can see that magnets work through air, but can they work through other materials? Place a piece of paper between two magnets. Has the pull or push become weaker? The answer is that there is no difference.

Magnets work through water just as they do through air, wood or any other material (Picture 4). The only material magnets will not work through is iron or steel.

▼ (Picture 3) The further apart the magnets are, the less they attract or repel.

Summary
- The same kind of magnet ends will repel each other.
- Different kinds of magnet ends attract each other.
- Magnets need to be close together to work.

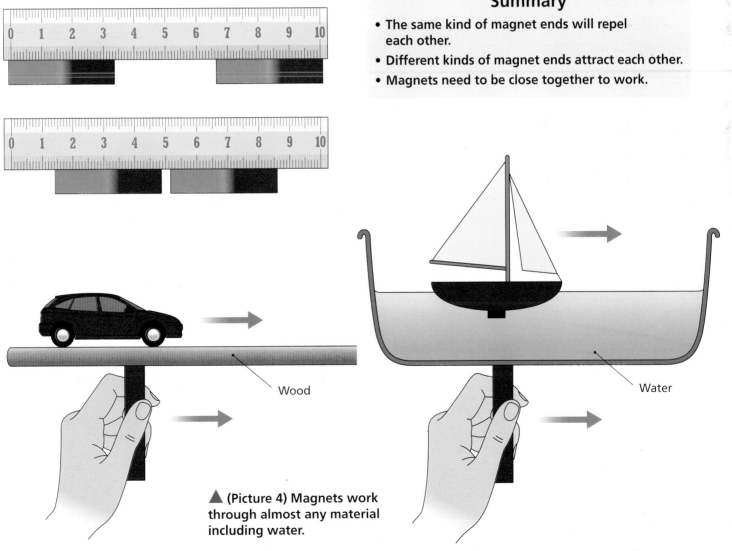

Wood

Water

▲ (Picture 4) Magnets work through almost any material including water.

Weblink: www.science-at-school.com

Seeing how a magnet works

Tiny pieces of iron and steel can be used to show where a magnet is working.

This page and the next page show demonstrations that allow you to see the effects of the invisible power of a magnet.

Floating on air

If you tie a paperclip to a thread and then hold it close to a magnet, the paperclip will tug on the thread as it is pulled by the magnet.

If you move the magnet away from the paperclip, the paperclip will follow and seem to float in the air.

Make patterns of iron

How far does magnetism affect things? If you have some very fine pieces of iron (called iron filings) you can find out.

Support a thin sheet of cardboard by placing books underneath the corners.

Now sprinkle the iron filings onto the cardboard so that they make a thin, even coating (Picture 1).

Bring the magnet under the cardboard and move it around the underside. The filings will follow as if by magic, making swirling patterns.

When the filings get clumped up, take the magnet away, shake the cardboard to spread the filings out and try again.

▲ (Picture 1) How iron filings can be used to find out how far a magnet works.

See the powerful ends of a magnet

This time, place a bar magnet on a table and place the cardboard on top of the magnet (Picture 2). Make sure the cardboard stays level. Now slowly sprinkle iron filings on the cardboard. Some of them will move about and form trails. Gently tap one corner of the cardboard

Weblink: www.science-at-school.com

▼ **(Picture 2) Tracing patterns of a bar magnet.**

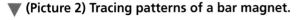

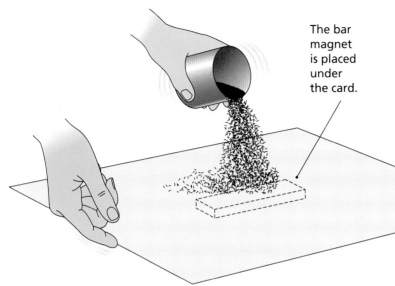

The bar magnet is placed under the card.

▼ **(Picture 3) The iron filings in this picture are tracing the pattern of forces surrounding a bar magnet (the red rectangle).**

and the filings will line up into a pattern, such as the one in Picture 3.

What you are seeing is the way the magnet pulls. See how trails go in and out of where the ends of the magnet are. Where the trails go in and out are the most powerful parts of the magnet.

Summary

- **The way a magnet pulls at things around it can be seen using iron filings.**
- **The most powerful parts of the magnet are at the ends.**

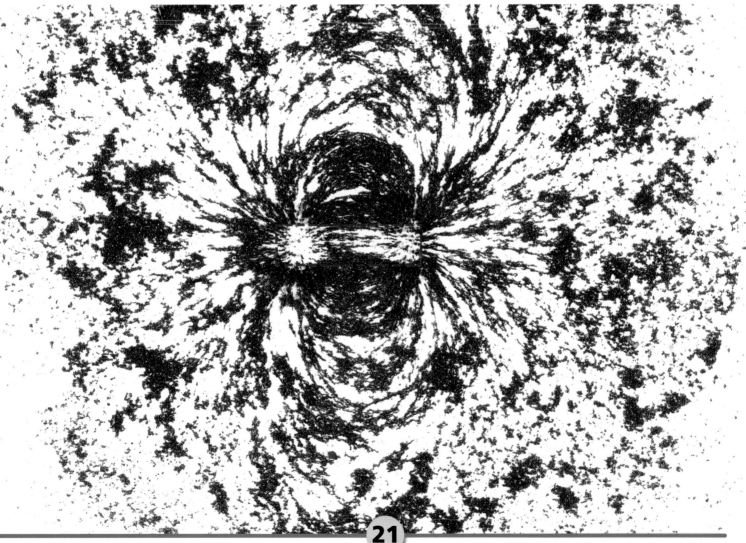

Weblink: www.science-at-school.com

The Earth as a magnet

The Earth behaves just as if it were a giant bar magnet.

Since ancient times, people have known that some black rocks had mysterious properties. These rocks could attract a piece of iron to them. Some people were afraid that if they sailed their ships too close to such black rocks then all of the iron nails would be pulled from the ships and they would sink.

Lodestone

This was, of course, not true. But they did find out some useful things about this strange rock. For example, if a small sliver of the rock was hung from a piece of string, then they saw two things:

▶ The stone always turned until it faced one particular way.
▶ One particular end always pointed north.

They called this rock lodestone (Picture 1), meaning leading stone, because it would help lead them home.

Compass

People found that needles and other pieces of iron or steel that had been magnetised would work in the same way

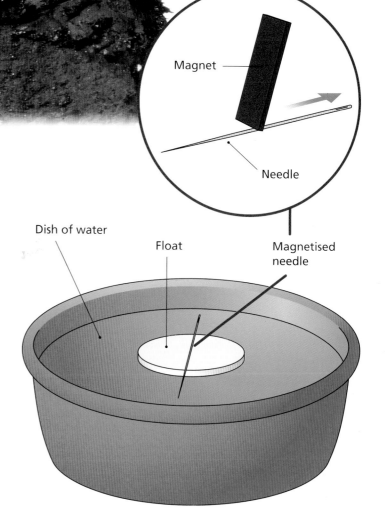

◀ (Picture 1) Some rocks, such as this one, are magnetic. This rock has been dipped in iron filings. The filings are not stuck on. They are simply held there by magnetism. This kind of rock is called lodestone.

Magnet

Needle

Dish of water

Float

Magnetised needle

▲ (Picture 2) You can make a compass for yourself using a needle or thin nail, a piece of foam to act as a float and a dish of water. Magnetise the needle or nail as described on page 16, then put it onto the float and watch it turn. Use a shop-bought compass to check that it faces north.

Weblink: www.science-at-school.com

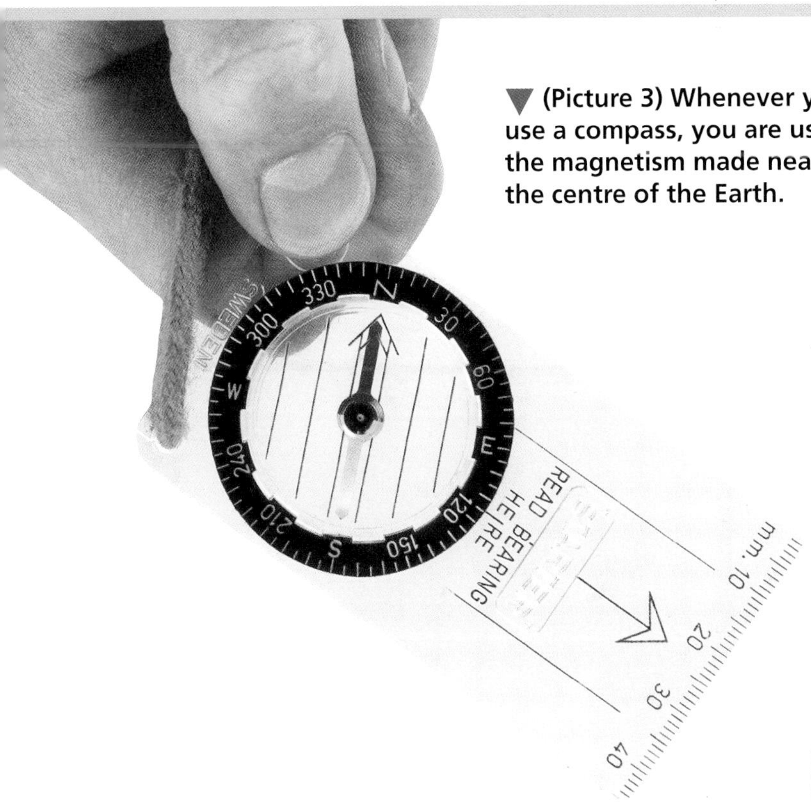

(Picture 3) Whenever you use a compass, you are using the magnetism made near the centre of the Earth.

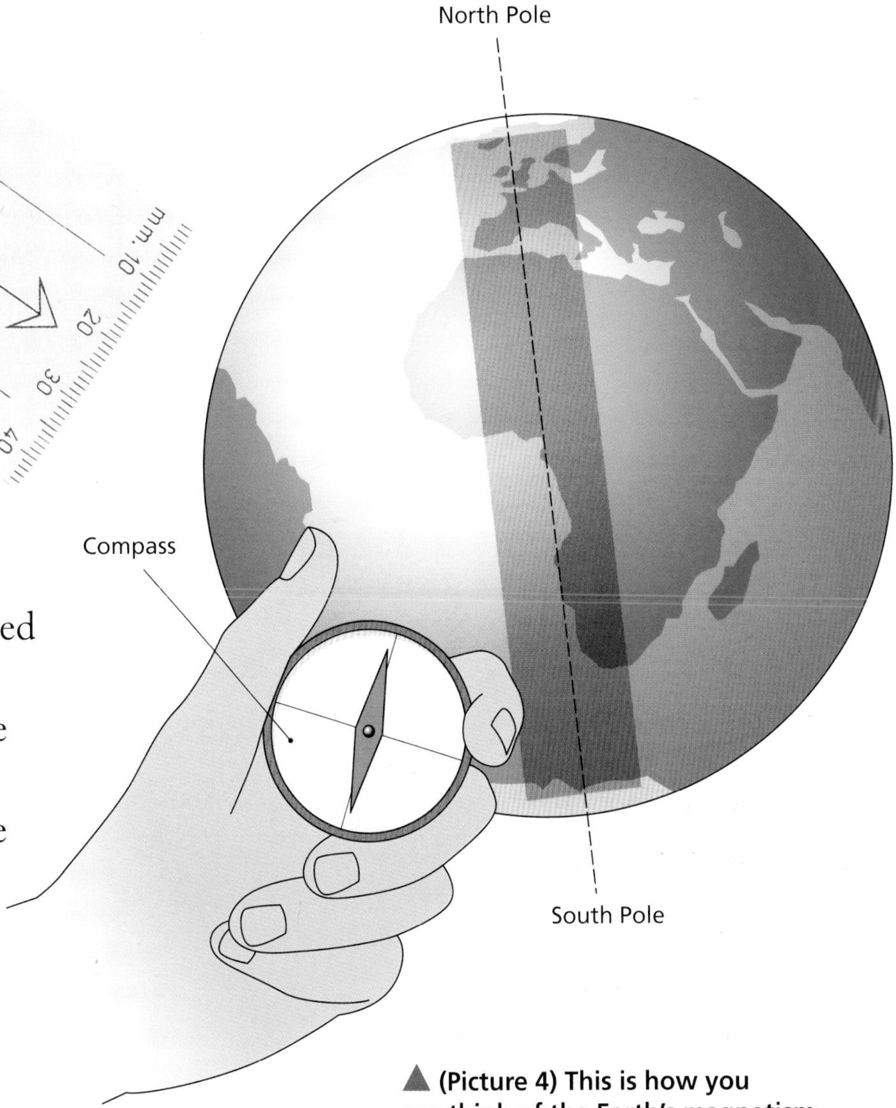

North Pole

Compass

South Pole

(Picture 2). If they put a magnetised needle on a piece of material and floated it on water then the needle would turn to face north. They had invented the **COMPASS**. Some modern compasses still float on water, but many simply turn in air (Picture 3).

The Earth

A compass only works because the magnetism in the compass needle is affected by magnetism in the Earth. Scientists have found that the centre of the Earth is made from iron, and this is what makes the Earth into a giant magnet. It works just as though there was a giant bar magnet inside (Picture 4).

(Picture 4) This is how you can think of the Earth's magnetism. However, there is no bar inside the Earth. All of the magnetism is at the ball-shaped centre of the Earth.

Summary
- The Earth is a giant magnet.
- A swinging magnet is called a compass.
- A compass is turned by the Earth's magnetism so that it always faces north.

Weblink: www.science-at-school.com

Index

Science@School

Science@School is a series published by Atlantic Europe Publishing Company Ltd.

Atlantic Europe Publishing

Teacher's Guide
There is a Teacher's Guide to accompany this book, available only from the publisher.

CD-ROMs
There are browser-based CD-ROMs containing information to support the series. They are available from the publisher.

Dedicated Web Site
There's more information about other great Science@School packs and a wealth of supporting material available at our dedicated web site:

www.science-at-school.com

First published in 2002 by
Atlantic Europe Publishing Company Ltd

Copyright © 2002
Atlantic Europe Publishing Company Ltd

All rights reserved. No part of this publication may be reproduced, stored in a retrieval system, or transmitted in any form or by any means, electronic, mechanical, photocopying, recording or otherwise, without prior permission of the publisher.

Author
Brian Knapp, BSc, PhD

Educational Consultant
Peter Riley, BSc, C Biol, MI Biol, PGCE

Art Director
Duncan McCrae, BSc

Senior Designer
Adele Humphries, BA, PGCE

Editor
Lisa Magloff, BA

Illustrations
David Woodroffe

Designed and produced by
EARTHSCAPE EDITIONS

Reproduced in Malaysia by
Global Colour

Printed in Hong Kong by
Wing King Tong Company Ltd

Science@School
Volume 3E *Springs and magnets*
A CIP record for this book is available from the British Library.
Paperback ISBN 1 86214 116 9

Picture credits
All photographs are from the Earthscape Editions photolibrary.

This product is manufactured from sustainable managed forests. For every tree cut down at least one more is planted.